W9-BTK-337

Going to Work SCHOOL EDITION · Going to Work SCHOOL EDITION · Going to Work SCHOOL EDITION · Going to
SCHOOL EDITION · Going to Work SCHOOL EDITION · Going to Work SCHOOL EDITION · Going to
Going to Work SCHOOL EDITION · Going to Work SCHOOL EDITION · Going to Work
SCHOOL EDITION · Going to Work SCHOOL EDITION · Going to Work SCHOOL EDITION · HOOL E
Going To Work
SCHOOL EDITION

Principals

ABDO
Publishing Company

A Buddy **Book** by
Julie Murray

VISIT US AT
www.abdopublishing.com

Published by ABDO Publishing Company, 8000 West 78th Street, Edina, Minnesota 55439.

Printed in the United States of America, North Mankato, Minnesota.
022010
092010

PRINTED ON RECYCLED PAPER

Coordinating Series Editor: Rochelle Baltzer
Editor: Sarah Tieck
Contributing Editors: Heidi M.D. Elston, Megan M. Gunderson, BreAnn Rumsch, Marcia Zappa
Graphic Design: Maria Hosley
Cover Photograph: Michael P. Goecke.
Interior Photographs/Illustrations: *AP Photo*: Terrance Armstard/The News-Star (p. 12), Nick Arroyo/Atlanta Journal-Constitution (p. 13), Ernest K. Bennett (p. 25), Heather Clark (p. 5), Norm Dettlaff/Las Cruces Sun-News (p. 30), Joseph C. Garza/Tribune Star (p. 29), Mead Gruver (p. 17), Bob King/The Duluth News-Tribune (p. 21), John Smock (p. 23), Evan Vucci (p. 27); *Corbis*: ©Ralf-Finn Hestoft (p. 9), ©Kim Kulish (p. 15); Michael P. Goecke (pp. 5, 7, 19); *iStockphoto*: ©iStockphoto.com/keeweeboy (p. 11).

Library of Congress Cataloging-in-Publication Data

Murray, Julie, 1969-
  Principals / Julie Murray.
    p. cm. -- (Going to work. School edition)
  ISBN 978-1-61613-508-9
  1. School principals--Juvenile literature. 2. School management and organization--Juvenile literature. I. Title.
  LB2831.9.M87 2011
  371.2'012--dc22
                                                                        2009050816

Contents

People at Work

Going to work is an important part of life. At work, people use their skills to complete tasks and earn money.

There are many different types of workplaces. Schools, factories, and offices are all workplaces.

Principals work in schools. They are school leaders. Principals set educational **goals** and make sure schools run properly. Their work helps students succeed.

A principal works with all the students who attend his or her school.

Office Work

A principal has an office at a school. He or she works and has meetings there. It is usually near the front of the building.

Principals work with everyone at a school. They hire and **evaluate** teachers and other **staff**. And, they meet with students and parents.

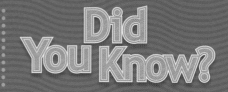

Some large schools have assistant principals. They help with some of the principal's work. And if the principal is gone, they are in charge.

Principals have long workdays. They often work on the computer.

7

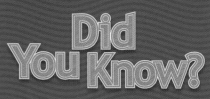
Principals often work more than 40 hours per week. They start work before the school day begins. Sometimes, they attend after-school events or meetings.

Each day brings different jobs. But, principals do some tasks regularly. They often check in with **staff** and visit classrooms.

Principals visit classrooms to meet and get to know students.

Job Training

To become a principal, a person usually must have an advanced **degree**. To earn the degree, he or she studies education and **administration**.

Many principals start out as teachers. This prepares them for work as school administrators.

When people earn degrees, they attend a graduation ceremony. This special event honors their hard work.

In most states, a principal must have a **license**. Some states also require a principal to pass a test.

Principals spend a lot of time working with other people. Being friendly is an important job skill.

Principals help teachers improve their work performance. This is part of being an administrator.

After they are hired, principals may continue to take classes. They learn about important changes and new ideas in **administration** and education.

A Day at Work

Principals get to school before students arrive. They may do paperwork or attend early meetings.

Principals often greet students as they enter the school. They walk the halls and talk to students and teachers.

When the bell rings, the school day begins. Some principals make announcements to the entire school. They share important news and **information**.

14

Principals are in charge of keeping students safe. So, they may be with students outside or in the halls.

During the school day, principals may observe teachers giving lessons. Or, they may help teachers create plans for students with special needs.

Principals meet with other principals. Together, they set educational **goals** for their schools. Principals also meet with parents to share **information** about students.

Principals may help students when teachers are away for extra training.

All Year Long

Principals work throughout the year. Many work in the summer, when most students are on break.

During summer months, principals set **goals** and make plans for the coming year. They may hire new **staff** members. They also oversee workers as they prepare the school building for the year.

Principals hire staff for the school cafeteria.
They make sure the cafeteria runs smoothly.

Leading Learners

Every grade level has certain learning requirements. Principals make sure students meet these standards. One way to measure this is by giving students tests.

Principals look at test scores. Then, they work with teachers to help students improve. They may create new lesson plans. And, principals may order books or computer programs to aid learning.

Sometimes, principals do silly things to help
their students learn! This principal promised to
kiss a pig if her students met their reading goals.

Principals work directly with students to solve problems. A student struggling in class may meet with a principal. Or, if students are arguing, a principal might step in.

Principals also work with a student's parents. Sometimes, families need extra help. Principals connect them to services, such as child care.

Principals show parents how they can be included in their child's education.

HISTORY LESSON

Years ago, principals spent most of their time **managing** schools and **staffs**. They also worked with students to solve problems. Today, principals do all this and more.

In the past, principals worked to teach students about good choices. They still do this today!

Did You Know?

George W. Bush was the U.S. president from 2001 to 2009.

In 2002, President George W. Bush signed a new law. It is called No Child Left Behind. The law set specific learning standards for U.S. students.

This law changed the jobs of principals. Principals still work on **administration**. But today, much more of their time is spent on educational **goals**. They work hard to make sure every student learns and succeeds.

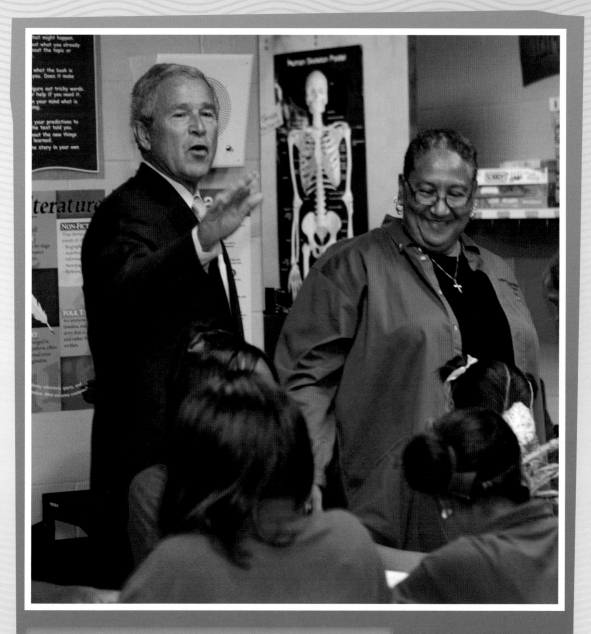

George W. Bush visited many schools when he was president. He was interested in improving education.

Helpful Leaders

Principals have an important job. They are trusted to keep schools running well. This makes it possible for students to succeed. School principals do special work that benefits their communities!

Principals are good leaders. Many students and teachers look up to them.

The School News

Around the World

In some U.S. schools, principals have a different name. They are called headmasters or headmistresses. These names are common in many other countries, such as England.

Is That a Fact?

One-room schoolhouses were common in the 1800s. These schools had no need for principals. The teachers did everything!

Important Words

administration (uhd-mih-nuh-STRAY-shuhn) the act or process of taking care of a school. An administrator is someone who does this.

degree a title given by a college to its students for completing their studies. An advanced degree, such as a master's or a doctorate, is earned by completing graduate school after college.

evaluate (ih-VAL-yuh-wayt) to decide the value or worth of.

goal something that a person works to reach or complete.

information (ihn-fuhr-MAY-shuhn) knowledge obtained from learning or studying something.

license (LEYE-suhnts) a paper or a card showing that someone is allowed to do something by law.

manage to look after or make decisions about.

staff a group of people who work for a place, such as a company, a school, or a church.

Web Sites

To learn more about principals, visit ABDO Publishing Company online. Web sites about principals are featured on our Book Links page. These links are routinely monitored and updated to provide the most current information available.

www.abdopublishing.com

31

Index